Writers

—— on ——

Writers

Writers
— ON —
Writers

COMPILED BY
GRAHAM TARRANT

INTRODUCTION BY
JOHN UPDIKE

AURUM PRESS

FOR FRANCESCA LOUISE, WITH LOVE

FIRST PUBLISHED 1995 BY AURUM PRESS LIMITED

25 BEDFORD AVENUE, LONDON WC1B 3AT

A CATALOGUE RECORD FOR THIS BOOK IS AVAILABLE FROM
THE BRITISH LIBRARY.

ISBN 1 85410 318 0

DESIGNED BY DESIGN/SECTION, FROME
PRINTED BY REGENT PUBLISHING SERVICES LTD
IN HONG KONG

INTRODUCTION

Writers, those self-consuming solitaries, are fascinated by other writers. They know how curious and, in the sought-for fusion of word and thing, arduous the trick of their trade is, and yet how commonly available the tools are – a little learning, a little imagination. They eye each other with a vigorous jealousy and suspicion. They are swift to condemn and dismiss, as a means of keeping the field from getting too crowded. To Rebecca West, Evelyn Waugh was "a disgusting common little man." Thomas Carlyle confided to his diary of Charles Lamb, "A more pitiful, rickety, gasping, staggering, stammering tomfool I do not know." According to Lord Byron Robert Southey was "a dirty, lying rascal," and according to Robert Southey Percy Bysshe Shelley was "a liar and a cheat" who "paid no regard to truth, nor to any kind of moral obligation."

All these condemnations are skimmed from the first pages of Graham Tarrant's piquant and savory anthology. Such keen appraisals are based, one gathers, not just on perusal of a rival's words but on personal acquaintance, and in this respect the English writers have an advantage over their American counterparts, who inhabit a larger and less clubbable country. True, for a few years in the middle of the last century, the social circles of Hawthorne, Melville, and Emerson intersected; but of the three only Melville hungered for the rub of genius on genius. Hawthorne was a natural recluse and Emerson's relations with even his disciple Thoreau were a bit wary and lofty. Melville felt it a flaw in Emerson that he emanated "the insinuation that had he lived in those days when the world was made, he might have offered some valuable suggestions." The remark is coolly catty; cattiness in general eludes the heavy-pawed Americans. Emerson thumped Swinburne as "a perfect leper and a mere sodomite," Pound likened Chesterton to "a vile scum on a pond," and Dorothy Parker put away Somerset Maugham with "That old lady is a crashing bore." Henry James came closer to the right drawled note in his description of Carlyle as "the same old sausage, fizzing and sputtering in his own grease." James Russell Lowell's verdict on Pope, "careless thinking carefully versified," is a handsome put-down, though it doesn't make us laugh with its justice, as does Cyril Connolly's saying of George Orwell, "He would not blow his nose without moralising on the state of the handkerchief industry."

A writer, I have found, takes less comfort in being praised (the reviewer was fooled or lazy, possibly) than in a colleague's being panned. I enjoyed this assemblage of choice quotations an indecent amount, considering that nine-tenths of them are uncomplimentary or adverse. Writers, themselves practitioners of the mysteries of the literary trade, are inhibited by no mystique or timid reverence; it takes one to know one, as the saying goes. How beautifully *seen*, for example, is V.S. Pritchett's evocation of William Butler Yeats descending the stairs with his "short, pale and prescient nose" and a birdlike air "suggesting one of the milder swans of Coole and an exalted sort of blindness." Just above it on page 41 we have Edith Sitwell's very vivifying vision of D.H. Lawrence as "a plaster gnome on a stone toadstool in some suburban garden" and "a bad self-portrait by Van Gogh," with "a rather matted, dank appearance…as if he had just returned from spending an uncomfortable night in a very dark cave." Sitwell in turn was seen through Dylan Thomas's Blakeian eyes as "a poisonous thing of a woman, lying, concealing, flipping, plagiarising, misquoting, and being as clever a crooked publicist as ever." Her latest book is to him her "latest piece of virgin dung." To Samuel Johnson, Rousseau was simply "a very bad man."

From the admission that a good writer might be a scoundrel it is but a short step to the speculation that a writer is necessarily something of a scoundrel. A raffish and bitter scent clings to the inky profession. Seeing truly and giving the human news frankly are both discourtesies, at least to those in the immediate vicinity. The writer's value to mankind irresistibly manifests itself at some remove of space and, often, time. In the meantime, his or her contemporaries are apt to see in him or her a bore, a charlatan, a sneak, an idler, a snob, a drunk. It is not just social friction or personal envy that gives the sharp edge to so many of the following appraisals; writers, with their own inside experience of poetry and fiction, are especially quick to sniff out the personality behind the writings of another. Noël Coward detected in John Osborne "a conceited, calculating young man blowing a little trumpet."

Osborne, having viewed two of Shaw's greatest, most eloquent plays, pronounced him "the most fraudulent, inept writer of Victorian melodramas ever to gull a timid critic or fool a dull public." Neither pronouncement is fair, but then fairness becomes a secondary issue on any battlefield.

Writing is life and death to writers. An intense competition rages for the cool limelight of literary publicity and for the never large and presently dwindling body of serious readers. To be sure, there are some generous words in this array: Jack London expresses his surprising debt to Kipling, Valéry his startlingly high opinion of Poe, Tolstoy his tender feelings toward Chekhov, Raymond Chandler his respect for Somerset Maugham. But the section "Praise Be!" is a brief, bland course almost lost in the midst of this peppery feast, affording the reader a chance to refresh his palate for the next wave of stinging delicacies. Not even Virgil, Dante, Shakespeare, and Goethe are spared the hot sauce.

A greater number of acute comments on literary matters and persons will scarcely be found in six dozen tomes of studious criticism. Mr Tarrant is to be complimented upon his locating in the vast gravel-beds of word-minded words so many trenchant, picturesque, witty, and heartfelt gems.

John Updike

Charact**e**r **S**tudies

He was (or rather had been) of a clear and faire skin; his habit was very plaine. I have heard Mr Lacy, the Player, say that he was wont to weare a coate like a coachman's coate, with slitts under the arme-pitts. He would many times exceed in drinke (Canarie was his beloved liquor) then he would tumble home to bed, and, when he had thoroughly perspired, then to studie.

JOHN AUBREY ON BEN JONSON,
Brief Lives

The greatest difficulty that occurs in analysing his character is to discover by what depravity of intellect he took delight in revolving ideas from which almost every other mind shrinks with disgust.

SAMUEL JOHNSON ON JONATHAN SWIFT,
Lives of the English Poets

He was compassionate both by nature and principle, and always ready to perform offices of humanity; but when he was provoked (and very small offences were sufficient to provoke him), he would prosecute his revenge with the utmost acrimony till his passion subsided. His friendship was therefore of little value; for though he was zealous in the support or vindication of those whom he loved, yet it was always dangerous to trust him, because he considered himself as discharged by the first quarrel from all ties of honour or gratitude, and would betray those secrets which in the warmth of confidence had been imparted to him.

SAMUEL JOHNSON ON RICHARD SAVAGE,
Lives of the English Poets

You think I like flattery and so I do; but a little too much always disgusts me: that fellow Richardson, on the contrary, could not be contented to sail quietly down the stream of reputation, without longing to taste the froth from every stroke of the oar.

SAMUEL JOHNSON ON SAMUEL RICHARDSON

With a lumber of learning and some strong parts, Johnson was an odious and mean character... His manners were sordid, supercilious, and brutal; his style ridiculously bombastic and vicious; and, in one word, with all the pedantry he had all the gigantic littleness of a country schoolmaster.

HORACE WALPOLE ON SAMUEL JOHNSON

The very look of Boswell seems to have signified so much. In that cocked nose, partly in triumph over his weaker fellow-

creatures, partly to snuff-up the smell of coming pleasure, and
scent it from afar; in those bag-cheeks, hanging like half-filled
wine-skins, still able to contain more; in that coarsely-protruded
shelf-mouth, that fat dewlapped chin; in all this, who sees not
sensuality, pretension, boisterous imbecility enough?...
Unfortunately, on the other hand, what great and genuine good
lay in him was nowise so self-evident.

THOMAS CARLYLE ON JAMES BOSWELL

Mamma says she was then the prettiest, silliest, most affected,
husband-hunting butterfly she ever remembers: and a friend of
mine, who visits her now, says that she has stiffened into the
most perpendicular, precise, taciturn piece of "single
blessedness" that ever existed, and that, till *Pride and Prejudice*
showed what a precious gem was hidden in that unbending case,
she was no more regarded in society than a poker or a fire-
screen, or any other thin upright piece of wood or iron that fills
its corner in peace and quietness. The case is very different
now: she is still a poker — but a poker of whom everyone is
afraid.

MARY RUSSELL MITFORD ON JANE AUSTEN,
letter to Sir William Elford, 3 April 1815

His nature was kind and his sentiments noble: but in him the rage
of free enquiry and private judgement amounted to a species of
madness. Whatever was new, untried, unheard of, unauthorised,
exerted a kind of fascination over his mind. The examples of the
world, the opinion of others, instead of acting as a check upon

him, served but to impel him forward with double velocity in his wild and hazardous career. Spurning the world of realities, he rushed into the world of nonentities and contingencies, like air into a vacuum. If a thing was old and established, this was with him a certain proof of its having no solid foundation to rest upon: if it was new, it was good and right.

WILLIAM HAZLITT ON PERCY BYSSHE SHELLEY

He was a liar and a cheat; he paid no regard to truth, nor to any kind of moral obligation.

ROBERT SOUTHEY ON PERCY BYSSHE SHELLEY

Mr Cobbett is great in attack, not in defence: he cannot fight an uphill battle. He will not bear the least punishing. If anyone turns upon him (which few people like to do) he immediately turns tail. Like an overgrown schoolboy, he is so used to have it all his own way that he cannot submit to anything like competition or a struggle for the mastery: he must lay on all the blows and take none... Whenever he has been set upon, he has slunk out of the controversy.

WILLIAM HAZLITT ON WILLIAM COBBETT,
Table Talk

The miscreant Hazlitt continues, I have heard, his abuse of Southey, Coleridge and myself in the *Examiner*. I hope that you do not associate with the fellow; he is not a proper person to be admitted into respectable society, being the most perverse and malevolent creature that ill-luck has thrown in my way. Avoid him.

WILLIAM WORDSWORTH,
letter to Benjamin Robert Haydon

His manners are to 99 in 100 singularly repulsive.

SAMUEL TAYLOR COLERIDGE ON WILLIAM HAZLITT

You may make what I say here as public as you please – more particularly to Southey, whom I look upon, and will say as publicly, to be a dirty, lying rascal; and will prove it in ink – or in his blood, if I did not believe him to be too much of a poet to risk it.

LORD BYRON ON ROBERT SOUTHEY,
letter to John Murray, 24 November 1818

Wordsworth rather dull. I see he is a man to *hold forth*; one who does not understand the *give and take* of conversation.

THOMAS MOORE,
Journal, 25 October 1820

Charles Lamb I do verily believe to be in some considerable degree insane. A more pitiful, rickety, gasping, staggering, stammering tomfool I do not know. He is witty by denying truisms and abjuring good manners... Poor Lamb! Poor England, when such a despicable abortion is named genius!

THOMAS CARLYLE,
Diary, 1831

Flaubert, on condition that one leaves the centre of the stage to him and resigns oneself to catching cold from all the windows he keeps throwing open, is a very pleasant companion. He has a jovial gaiety and a childlike laugh which are contagious; and everyday contact develops in him a certain gruff affectionateness which is not without charm.

EDMOND GONCOURT,
Journal, 21 September 1878

Her talk was marvellous, much better than her writing, especially when she was telling of things that she was going to write, but when she spoke about people she was envious, dark, and full of alarming penetration in discovering what they least wished known and whatever was bad in their characteristics.

BERTRAND RUSSELL ON KATHERINE MANSFIELD,
Autobiography 1914-44

One could always baffle Conrad by saying "humour". It was one of our damned English tricks he had never learned to tackle.

H.G.WELLS ON JOSEPH CONRAD

At a certain stage in drunkenness he gave himself and others the illusion of completely painless brilliance; words poured out of him, puns, metaphors, epigrams, visions; but soon the high spirits would be mingled with obsessions – "See that man staring at us, I think he's a detective" – and then the violence would start all over again, to be followed next day by the repentance that became a form of boasting. In this repeated process there was no longer a free hour for writing down his poems, or a week or a month in which to revise them.

MALCOLM COWLEY ON HART CRANE

Between being dangerous when drunk and eating humble pie when sober, I preferred Scott dangerous. An alcoholic is much more bearable when he's like Brendan Behan, roistering his way through to a tragic end, than for his life to fade out, as Scott's did, in one long, dull apologia.

ANITA LOOS ON SCOTT FITZGERALD

Of all the English writers I have known, he was the most honest, the frankest, the one least afraid of telling the truth. If he often offended public opinion, that is chiefly because English public opinion feeds itself with cant and humbug. He had not more dirty linen than most other authors, but, with a kind of innocence, he did his laundry work in the open. His genius was entirely literary, not scientific, but his early training, his discovery of a wide rich world through science, gave him permanently the air of a man making some hasty last-minute experiments in a lab. He was an artist gasping for breath in a scientific climate.

J.B.PRIESTLEY ON H.G.WELLS,
Margin Released

While most schoolboys dreamt of becoming engine-drivers or cattle-punchers, little Malcolm dreamt of becoming an alcoholic. And the dream came true. Excluding a few dry-outs, in hospitals and prisons, and the very occasional self-imposed prohibition, Malcolm Lowry was shit-faced for 35 years.

MARTIN AMIS

So you've been reviewing Edith Sitwell's latest piece of virgin dung, have you? Isn't she a poisonous thing of a woman, lying, concealing, flipping, plagiarising, misquoting, and being as clever a crooked publicist as ever.

DYLAN THOMAS,
letter to Glyn Jones, December 1934

Lewis's taste in *light* literature was that of a Victorian schoolboy. His *serious* literary taste was also nineteenth century, but that of a mid-nineteenth-century scholar and man of letters. He liked the grand, the noble, or the Romantic. Virgil, Homer, Milton, also Spenser, Malory etc – though he also did get a great deal of pleasure from writers as different as Lamb and Jane Austen. But his taste did stop about 1890.

DAVID CECIL ON C.S.LEWIS,
letter to Humphrey Carpenter, 1978

Papa possessed to an unusual degree the power of making other people want to please him – not just in the relatively undemanding sense of winning his approval, but of keeping him happy in a hundred ways, for instance sending him presents of pictures and artefacts, rare wines and delicacies; more particularly, he sent family and friends into the world to supply him with information and gossip to keep his imagination fed. Nothing ever happened to me while he was alive but I mentally sub-edited it into a report which would be sent to him in my next letter.

AUBERON WAUGH ON EVELYN WAUGH,
Will This Do?

A disgusting common little man – he had never been taught how to avoid being offensive.

REBECCA WEST ON EVELYN WAUGH

Jim, you were always a gentleman, even with assholes.

WILLIAM STYRON ON JAMES JONES

I only regret we never met, for friends found him a good companion, a fine drinking partner, and fun to cruise with.

GORE VIDAL ON YUKIO MISHIMA

CRITICAL COMMENT

The poems of Milton betray a narrowness of education and a degeneracy of habit. His theological quibbles and perplexed speculations are daily equalled and excelled by the most abject enthusiasts, and if we consider him as a prose writer, he has neither the learning of a scholar nor the manners of a gentleman. There is no force in his reasonings, no eloquence in his style, and no taste in his composition.

OLIVER GOLDSMITH

We have lately seen the whole of Herrick's poems published, a coarse-minded and beastly writer, whose dunghill, when the few flowers that grew there had been transplanted, ought never to have been disturbed. Those flowers are indeed beautiful and perennial; but they should have been removed from the filth and ordure in which they are buried.

ROBERT SOUTHEY ON ROBERT HERRICK,

Commonplace Books

I never felt very easy about Jane Austen: I think she made a tremendous, far-reaching decision to leave certain things out. She forfeited passion for wit, and I think that led her to collude with certain little stratagems which are horrifying in real life. She wrote about getting husbands.

ANITA BROOKNER

Also read again, and for the third time at least, Miss Austen's very finely written novel of *Pride and Prejudice*. That young lady had a talent for describing the involvements and feelings and characters of ordinary life, which is to me the most wonderful I ever met with. The Big Bow-wow strain I can do myself like any now going; but the exquisite touch, which renders ordinary commonplace things and characters interesting, from the truth of the description, is denied me. What a pity such a gifted creature died so early!

SIR WALTER SCOTT,
Journal, 14 March 1826

Walter Scott has no business to write novels, especially good ones. It is not fair. He has fame and profit enough as a poet, and should not be taking the bread out of other people's mouths. I do not like him, and do not mean to like *Waverley* if I can help it – but fear I must.

JANE AUSTEN,
letter to her niece, September 1814

You've got to be one of two ages to appreciate Scott. When you're eighteen you can read *Ivanhoe*, and you want to wait until you are ninety to read some of the rest. It takes a pretty well-regulated abstemious critic to live ninety years.

MARK TWAIN ON SIR WALTER SCOTT,
Speech, 20 November 1900

I have no patience with the sort of trash you send me out by way of books; except Scott's novels, and three or four other things, I never saw such work or works. Campbell is lecturing, Moore idling, Southey twaddling, Wordsworth driveling, Coleridge muddling, Joanna Baillie piddling, Bowles quibbling, squabbling, and sniveling.

LORD BYRON,
letter to John Murray, 12 September 1821

I am sorry that Coleridge has christened his *Ancient Marinere*, a *Poet's Reverie*; it is as bad as Bottom the Weaver's declaration that he is not a lion, but only the scenical representation of a lion. What new idea is gained by this title but one subversive of all credit – which the tale should force upon us – of its truth!

CHARLES LAMB,
letter to William Wordsworth, February 1801

If Mr Coleridge had not been the most impressive talker of his age, he would probably have been the finest writer; but he lays down his pen to make sure of an auditor, and mortgages the admiration of posterity for the stare of an idler.

WILLIAM HAZLITT

Never did I see such apparatus got ready for thinking, and so little thought. He mounts scaffolding, pulleys and tackle, gathers all the tools in the neighbourhood with labour, with noise, demonstration, precept, abuse, and sets – three bricks.

THOMAS CARLYLE ON SAMUEL TAYLOR COLERIDGE

Cooper's art has some defects. In one place in *Deerslayer*, and in the restricted space of two-thirds of a page, Cooper has scored 114 offences against literary art out of a possible 115. It breaks the record.

MARK TWAIN ON JAMES FENIMORE COOPER

I wish her characters would talk a little less like the heroes and heroines of police reports.

GEORGE ELIOT ON CHARLOTTE BRONTË

[Reviewing *Leaves of Grass*] Under the dirty clumsy paws of a harper whose plectrum is a muck-rake, any tune will become a chaos of discords... Mr Whitman's Eve is a drunken apple-woman, indecently sprawling in the slush and garbage of the gutter amid the rotten refuse of her overturned fruit-stall: but

Mr Whitman's Venus is a Hottentot wench under the influence of cantharides and adulterated rum.

ALGERNON CHARLES SWINBURNE ON WALT WHITMAN

His style is chaos illumined by flashes of lightning. As a writer he has mastered everything except language: as a novelist he can do everything, except tell a story: as an artist he is everything except articulate.

OSCAR WILDE ON GEORGE MEREDITH,
The Decay of Living

[After reading Tolstoy's first published work, *Childhood*] I like Leo Tolstoy enormously, but in my opinion he won't write much of anything else (though I can be wrong!).

FYODOR DOSTOEVSKY

Thank you for making me read Tolstoy's novel [*War and Peace*, in three volumes]. It's first rate. What a painter and what a psychologist! The first two are sublime; but the third goes terribly to pieces. He repeats himself and he philosophises! In fact the man, the author, the Russian are visible, whereas up until then one had seen only Nature and Humanity.

GUSTAVE FLAUBERT,
letter to Ivan Turgenev, 21 January 1880

That's the trouble with James. You get bored with him finally. He lived in the time of four-wheelers, and no bombs, and the problems then seemed a bit special and separate. That's one reason you feel restless reading him. James is like – well, I had a bulldog once who used to drag rails around, enormous ones, six-, eight-, twelve-foot rails. He'd love to get them in the middle and you'd hear him growling out there, trying to bring the thing home... Well, he'd start to get these things in the garden gate, everything finely balanced, you see, and then *crash*, he'd come up against the gate posts. He'd get it through finally, but I had that feeling in some of the James novels: that he was trying to get that rail through a gate not wide enough for it.

JAMES THURBER ON HENRY JAMES,
Paris Review interview

Henry James would have been vastly improved as a novelist by a few whiffs from the Chicago stockyards.

H.L.MENCKEN

Reading Proust is like bathing in someone else's dirty water.

ALEXANDER WOOLLCOTT

From the point of view of literature Mr Kipling is a genius who drops his aspirates. From the point of view of life, he is a reporter who knows vulgarity better than any one has ever known it. Dickens knew its clothes and its comedy. Mr Kipling knows its essence and its seriousness. He is our first authority on the second-rate, and has seen marvellous things through keyholes, and his backgrounds are real works of art.

OSCAR WILDE,
The Critic as Artist

Virginia Woolf herself never got used to the fact that if you write books some people are bound to be rude about them.

ANTHONY POWELL

Hemingway's tragedy as an artist is that he has not had the versatility to run away fast enough from his imitators. The talkies that facilitated his success brought on a flood of talkie-novels, the trick of being tough, the knack of writing entirely in dialogue interrupted only by a few sentimental landscapes caught on and with each bad copy the prestige of the original was affected. A Picasso would have done something different; Hemingway could only indulge in invective against his critics – and do it again.

CYRIL CONNOLLY,
Enemies of Promise

[In response to some hefty criticism of Hemingway's new novel, *Across the River and into the Trees*] The man who wrote some of the pieces in *Men Without Women* and *The Sun Also Rises* and some of the African stuff (and some – most – of all the rest of it too for that matter) does not need defending, because the ones who throw the spitballs didn't write the pieces in *Men Without Women* and *The Sun Also Rises* and the African pieces and the rest of it, and the ones who didn't write *Men Without Women* and *The Sun Also Rises* and the African pieces and the rest of it don't have anything to stand on while they throw the spitballs.

WILLIAM FAULKNER,
letter to Time, 13 November 1950

[**C**ommenting on E.M.Forster's claim that his major characters sometimes took over and dictated the course of his novels] My knowledge of Mr Forster's works is limited to one novel which I dislike, and anyway it was not he who fathered that trite little whimsy about characters getting out of hand, it is as old as the quills, although, of course, one sympathises with his people if they try to wriggle out of that trip to India or wherever he takes them.

VLADIMIR NABOKOV,
Paris Review interview

I do not want Miss Mannin's feelings to be hurt by the fact that I have never heard of her. At the moment I am debarred from the pleasures of putting her in her place by the fact she has not got one.

EDITH SITWELL ON ETHEL MANNIN

There is not one Henry Miller, but twenty, and fifteen of those authors are very good. Of course, when Miller is bad, he may be the worst great writer ever to be bad.

NORMAN MAILER

[Reviewing *The Adventures of Wesley Jackson*] Once more Saroyan is full of love for the entire world. He loves the Germans, he loves the Japs, he loves the Bulgarians and Finns and Rumanians. The only people he can find to hate are the Americans. He forgives the Germans Dachau and Belsen without blinking an eye, but he cannot forgive the sergeant who assigned him to KP in New York City... It seems to me that a writer, no matter how far-fetched and fanciful he may be, should have some compulsion to present the truth.

IRWIN SHAW ON WILLIAM SAROYAN,
New York Times, 2 June 1946

His books and plays with their breathless pursuit of the very latest liberaloid cliché-problem, his improbable dialogue (only he himself apparently talks like his own characters), his limp watery prose are scarcely worth more than the sentence it takes to describe them. More precisely, perhaps, they would be worth no more than that sentence, except for the fact that they represent an ideal of literary achievement, a style and attitude and choice of subject of which a whole class of readers dream. Irwin Shaw is, in fact, a sociological touchstone.

LESLIE FIEDLER ON IRWIN SHAW,
Commentary, July 1956

She writes like a middle-aged French *roué*. She writes like Carl Jung dreaming he is Candide.

JOHN BARTH ON SUSAN SONTAG

He has no talent, except for writing essays. He has no interior sensitivity – he can't put himself into someone else's place – and except for *Myra Breckinridge*, he never really found his voice. Anybody could have written *Julian* or *Burr*.

TRUMAN CAPOTE ON GORE VIDAL

[Reviewing *Art and Lies*] Just as certain modern paintings do not want to be paintings but rather statements, so certain modern novels want to be paintings, or pieces of music, or sculptures; anything but a book, one of those lowly things they sell in airports. This is one of them. It might be an idea if Miss Winterson got out her brushes and set to, painting her masterpiece as soon as possible. Because the signs are, right now, that she certainly isn't ever going to write one.

JULIE BURCHILL ON JEANETTE WINTERSON,
The Spectator, London, June 1994

Dear Diary

Gibbon is an ugly, affected, disgusting fellow, and poisons our literary club for me. I class him among infidel wasps and venomous insects.

JAMES BOSWELL ON EDWARD GIBBON,

Diary, 1779

To dinner at Sir Walter Scott's. Was rather shocked at seeing and hearing Scott; both his looks and utterance, but particularly the latter, showing strongly the effects of paralysis. On looking over at Scott once or twice, was painfully struck by the utter vacancy of his look. How dreadful if he should live to survive that mighty mind of his! It seems hardly right to assemble company round him in this state. It is charming to see how Scott's good temper and good nature continue unchanged through the sad wreck of almost every thing else that belonged to him. The great object in sending him abroad is to disengage his mind from the strong wish to write by which he is haunted; eternally making efforts to produce something without being able to bring his mind collectively to bear upon it.

THOMAS MOORE,

Journal, 14 October 1831

I met Peacock; a very clever fellow, and a good scholar. I am glad to have an opportunity of being better acquainted with him. We had out Aristophanes, Aeschylus, Sophocles, and several other old fellows, and tried each other's quality pretty well. We are both strong enough in these matters for gentlemen.

**THOMAS BABINGTON MACAULAY ON
THOMAS LOVE PEACOCK,**

Journal, 31 December 1851

Zola really has nothing in him that he can call his own, and any reader who makes a thorough study of his work will be astonished at all he has taken from other writers in the way of types, characters, situations, scenes, endings, and even images and comparisons. That huge, awe-inspiring animal that he makes out of a factory, a barracks, or a shop, is a comparison taken from *Notre-Dame de Paris* which he uses again and again in all his lyrical works.

EDMOND GONCOURT,

Journal, 6 March 1887

I went on to a dinner at Sinclair Lewis's timed for 8 o'clock… Lewis has a habit of breaking into a discussion with long pieces of imaginary conversation between imaginary or real people of the place and period under discussion. Goodish, but too long, with accents, manner, and all complete. He will do this in any discussion; he will drag in a performance, usually full of oaths and blasphemy.

ARNOLD BENNETT,
Journal, 4 January 1924

Aldous Huxley is getting more and more into the habit of using such words as "inconceivable", "incredible", "fantastic". These three are his favourite words, and one of them comes into nearly every sentence. His general knowledge is extraordinarily good. In fact it is inconceivable, incredible, and fantastic.

ARNOLD BENNETT,
Journal, 14 February 1927

A nervous wreck named Beverley Nichols has arrived. Not a man of strong understanding. A mercenary, hypochondriacal, flibbertigibbet who doesn't take in one of six words addressed to him – but civil to old ladies.

EVELYN WAUGH,
Diary, 21 May 1944

I have also read *The Charioteer* by Miss Mary Renault. Oh dear, I do, do wish well-intentioned ladies would *not* write books about homosexuality. This one is turgid, unreal and so ghastly earnest... I'm sure the poor woman meant well but I wish she'd stick to recreating the glory that was Greece and not fuck about with dear old modern homos.

NOËL COWARD,
Diary, 6 August 1960

Betjeman's biography [*Summoned by Bells*]. John demonstrates how much more difficult it is to write blank verse than jingles and raises the question: *why* did he not go into his father's workshop? It would be far more honourable and useful to make expensive ashtrays than to appear on television, and just as lucrative.

EVELYN WAUGH,
Diary, December 1960

Hemingway shot himself yesterday morning. There was a great man. I remember walking down a street in Boston after reading a book of his, and finding the colour of the sky, the faces of strangers, and the smells of the city heightened and dramatized. The most important thing he did for me was to legitimatize manly courage, a quality that I had heard, until I came on his work, extolled by Scoutmasters and others who made it seem a fraud. He put down an immense vision of love and friendship, swallows and the sound of rain. There was never, in my time, anyone to compare with him.

JOHN CHEEVER,
Journal, 1961

Down to Work...

The man is a great jester, not a great humourist. He goes to work systematically and of cold blood; paints his face, puts on his ruff and motley clothes, and lays down his carpet and tumbles on it.

WILLIAM MAKEPEACE THACKERAY
ON LAURENCE STERNE,
The English Humourists

Flaubert is a great writer and a great stylist. He was more concerned with style than content. Content with him was like he would take an apple out of a basket and put it on a table and say, "Now I'm going to do this apple." I mean, I don't think he really gave a fuck about Madame Bovary. He cared how it all shaped itself, how real he could make it.

TRUMAN CAPOTE

It is, I think, the defect of George Eliot that she struggles too hard to do work that shall be excellent. She lacks ease. Latterly the signs of this have been conspicuous in her style, which has always been and is singularly correct, but which has become occasionally obscure from her too great desire to be pungent. It is impossible not to feel the struggle, and that feeling begets a flavour of affectation.

ANTHONY TROLLOPE

I think of him as a sculptor in snow, vast, perhaps luminous, but indistinct and brittle. Or if you prefer to think of clay – soft clay which is apt to crumble. You regard it with admiration, but you never fail to ask yourself inwardly how long it will last… The designs are great but there is very little material.

GEORGE MOORE ON FYODOR DOSTOEVSKY

Mr Walter Pater's style is, to me, like the face of some old woman who has been to Madame Rachel and had herself enamelled. The bloom is nothing but powder and paint and the odour is cherry-blossom. Mr Matthew Arnold's odour is as the faint sickliness of the hawthorn.

SAMUEL BUTLER

His humour lay in his point of view, his angle of vision and the truth with which he conveyed it. This often enabled people quite suddenly to see things as they are, and not as they had supposed them to be – a process which creates the peculiar sense of personal triumph which we call humour. The savage shout of exhultation modified down to our gurgling laugh greets the overthrow of the thing as it was. Mark Twain achieved this effect not by trying to be funny, but by trying to tell the truth.

STEPHEN LEACOCK

I am not saying anything against her morals, but judging from her style she ought to be here.

OSCAR WILDE ON MARIE CORELLI
(to the librarian in Reading gaol)

Been reading masses of Proust – you have to be awful sick and a little feverish to enjoy it – I think what people get is a cosy well to do feeling like a rich woman's appearance out that smells of flowers and lipstick and a little of gin and furniture polish – its surprizing how absolutely unarticulated his language is. You can't tell one sentence from the next. Half of the time I didn't know either where one began and another ended – because the punctuation is of the vaguest. He's not a hoax – but he's certainly no "maitre".

JOHN DOS PASSOS,
letter to Ernest Hemingway, 3 May 1933

Hammett took murder out of the parlor and put it in the alley where it belongs.

RAYMOND CHANDLER ON DASHIELL HAMMETT

Firbank has a beautiful precision of language, and he's also so very funny and melancholy; his evocation of landscape is as economical and beautiful as *haiku*. I've always thought that he was a plucky little bantamweight.

ANGELA CARTER ON RONALD FIRBANK

He could not write two lines of correct English... You may disregard grammar altogether, if you wish, but you cannot flop about as Hardy does.

GEORGE MOORE ON THOMAS HARDY

Gertrude Stein's prose is a cold, black suet-pudding. We can represent it as a cold suet-roll of fabulously reptilian length. Cut it at any point, it is the same thing; the same heavy, sticky, opaque mass all through, and all along.

WYNDHAM LEWIS

Her best word portraits are dervish dances of sheer hate, equivalent in the satisfaction they give her to the waxen images which people in olden days fashioned of their enemies in order, with exquisite pleasure, to stick pins into them.

ALEXANDER WOOLLCOTT ON DOROTHY PARKER,
While Rome Burns

The failure of academic literary criticism to take any account of Wodehouse's supreme mastery of the English language or the profound influence he has had on every worthwhile English novelist in the past 50 years demonstrates in better and conciser form than anything else how the Eng. Lit. industry is divorced from the subject it claims to study.

AUBERON WAUGH ON P.G.WODEHOUSE,
New Statesman, 21 February 1975

No one can write a sentence like White's, or successfully imitate it.

JAMES THURBER ON E.B.WHITE

He is the most perfect writer of my generation, he writes the best sentences word for word, rhythm upon rhythm. I would not have changed two words in *Breakfast at Tiffany's*.

NORMAN MAILER ON TRUMAN CAPOTE

Tom Wolfe is just not going to last. I love some of the things he's done, they're just terrific…but you won't think so in years to come. Because of his style. But if he hadn't used that style, nobody would have paid attention to him and he wouldn't have had the success that he had.

TRUMAN CAPOTE

FACE *to* FACE
ɟⱯCE *ɟo* ɟⱯCE

He is, indeed, very ill-favoured, is tall and stout, but stoops terribly. He is almost bent double. His mouth is almost constantly opening and shutting as if he were chewing. His body is in continual agitation, see-sawing up and down. His feet are never a moment quiet, and in short his whole person is in perpetual motion.

FANNY BURNEY ON SAMUEL JOHNSON

So morbid was his temperament, that he never knew the natural joy of a free and vigorous use of his limbs; when he walked, it was like the struggling gait of one in fetters; when he rode, he had no command or direction of his horse, but was carried as if in a balloon.

JAMES BOSWELL ON SAMUEL JOHNSON,
Life of Johnson

A loose, slack, not well-dressed youth met Mr Green and myself in a lane near Highgate. Green knew him, and spoke. It was Keats. He was introduced to me, and stayed a minute or so.

After he had left us a little way, he came back and said: "Let me carry away the memory, Coleridge, of having pressed your hand!" "There is death in that hand," I said to Green, when Keats was gone; yet this was, I believe, before the consumption showed itself distinctly.

SAMUEL TAYLOR COLERIDGE,
Table Talk

Keats' recollection of that same meeting:

Last Sunday I took a walk towards Highgate, and in the lane that winds by the side of Lord Mansfield's park I met Mr Green our Demonstrator at Guy's in conversation with Coleridge – I joined them, after enquiring by a look whether it would be agreeable – I walked with him at his alderman-after-dinner pace for near two miles I suppose. In those two miles he broached a thousand things – let me see if I can give you a list – Nightingales – Poetry – on Poetical Sensation – Metaphysics – Different genera and species of Dreams – Nightmare – a dream accompanied by a sense of touch – single and double touch – a dream related – first and second consciousness – the difference explained between will and volition – so say metaphysicians from a want of smoking the second consciousness – Monsters – the Kracken – Mermaids – Southey believes in them – Southey's belief too much diluted – a Ghost story – Good morning – I heard his voice as he came towards me – I heard it as he moved away – I heard it all the interval – if it may be called so.

JOHN KEATS,
letter to his brother, April 1819

He would often fall asleep in the day-time – dropping off in a moment – like an infant. He often quietly transferred himself from his chair to the floor, and slept soundly on the carpet, and in the winter upon the rug, basking in the warmth like a cat; and like a cat his little round head was roasted before a blazing fire. If anyone humanely covered the poor head to shield it from the heat, the covering was impatiently put aside in his sleep.

THOMAS JEFFERSON HOGG,
The Life of Percy Bysshe Shelley

He reminds one of some of Holbein's heads, grave, saturnine, with a slight indication of sly humour, kept under by the manners of the age or by the pretensions of the person. He has a peculiar sweetness in his smile, and great depth and manliness and a rugged harmony in the tones of his voice. His manner of reading his own poetry is particularly imposing; and in his favourite passages his eye beams with preternatural lustre, and the meaning labours slowly up from his swelling breast. No one who has seen him at these moments could go away with an impression that he was a "man of no mark or likelihood".

WILLIAM HAZLITT
ON WILLIAM WORDSWORTH

He is the *cleverest* man I ever met. I mean he impresses you more with the alertness of his various powers. His forces are all light infantry and light cavalry, and always in marching order. There are not many heavy pieces, but few *sappers* and *miners*, the scientific corps is deficient, and I fear there is no chaplain in the garrison.

RICHARD HENRY DANA ON CHARLES DICKENS

A large, thick-set sybil, dreamy and immobile, whose massive features, somewhat grim when seen in repose, were incongruously bordered by a hat, always in the height of Paris fashion, which in those days commonly included an immense ostrich feather; that was George Eliot. The contrast between the solemnity of the face and the frivolity of the headgear had something pathetic and provincial about it.

EDMUND GOSSE

On Monday (as you may have seen in *The Times*) I was invited to dinner at Victor Hugo's, and accordingly presented myself in a state of perturbation as well as delight before the greatest – I know – and I believe the best, man now living… He will be eighty-one in February, and walked upright and firm without a stick. His white hair is as thick as his dark eyebrows, and his eyes are as bright and clear as a little child's. After dinner, he drank my health with a little speech, of which – tho' I sat just opposite him – my accursed deafness prevented my hearing a single word.

ALGERNON CHARLES SWINBURNE,
letter to his mother, 26 November 1882

We could both wish that one's first impression of KM was not that she stinks like a – well civet cat that had taken to street walking. In truth, I'm a little shocked by her commonness at first sight; lines so hard and cheap. However, when this diminishes, she is so intelligent and inscrutable that she repays friendship.

VIRGINIA WOOLF ON KATHERINE MANSFIELD,
Diary, 11 October 1917

The first mate is a Pole called [Joseph] Conrad and is a capital chap, though queer to look at; he is a man of travel and experience in many parts of the world, and has a fund of yarns on which I draw freely.

JOHN GALSWORTHY,
letter from aboard the SS Torrens, en route from Australia, 23 April 1893

Mr Lawrence looked like a plaster gnome on a stone toadstool in some suburban garden. At the same time he bore some resemblance to a bad self-portrait by Van Gogh. He had a rather matted, dank appearance. He looked as if he had just returned from spending an uncomfortable night in a very dark cave, hiding, perhaps, in the darkness from something which, at the same time, he on his side was hunting.

EDITH SITWELL ON D.H.LAWRENCE,
Taken Care Of

Tall, with grey hair finely rumpled, a dandy with negligence in collar and tie and with the black ribbon dangling from the glasses on a short, pale and prescient nose – not long enough to be Roman yet not sharp enough to be a beak – Yeats came down the stairs towards me… His air was bird-like, suggesting one of the milder swans of Coole and an exalted sort of blindness. I had been warned that he would not shake hands.

V.S.Pritchett on William Butler Yeats,
Midnight Oil

I do not like your lips. They are quite straight, like the lips of one who has never told a lie.

Oscar Wilde on André Gide
(said at their first meeting)

In full face he looked as William Blake must have looked as a young man. He had full eyes – like those of Blake – giving at first the impression of being unseeing, but seeing all, looking over immeasurable distances.

Edith Sitwell on Dylan Thomas,
Taken Care Of

What I saw was a small man so short in the thighs that when he stood up he seemed smaller than when he was sitting down. He had a plum pudding of a body and a square head stuck on it with no intervening neck. His brown hair was parted exactly in the middle, and the two cowlicks touched his eyebrows. He had very light blue eyes small enough to show the whites above the irises, which gave him the earnestness of a gas jet when he talked, an air of resigned incredulity when he listened, and a merry acceptance of the human race and all its foibles when he grinned. He was dressed like the owner of a country hardware store.

ALISTAIR COOKE ON H.L.MENCKEN,
Six Men

Willie Maugham came in: like a dead man whose beard or moustache has grown a little grisly bristle after death. And his lips are drawn back like a dead man's. He has small ferret eyes. A look of suffering and malignity and meanness and suspicion.

VIRGINIA WOOLF ON SOMERSET MAUGHAM,
Diary, 1 November 1938

Eliot's conversation is gravely insistent. It does not give the impression of exceptional energy, but it has a kind of drive all its own, as it proceeds along its rigid lines. He cannot easily be interrupted or made to change the subject. I say it is a fine day, and Eliot replies gravely: "Yes, it is a fine day, but it was still finer yesterday –" with a faint hint in his voice that when I used the word "fine" of today I was not choosing the word altogether exactly. However, he continues about the weather: "If I remember, this time last year the lilac..." and then it is quite likely that if I have gone on listening carefully, out of this dry climate, there will suddenly flash a few words of poetry like a kingfisher's wing across the club-room conversation.

STEPHEN SPENDER ON T.S.ELIOT,
World Within World

I was startled by O'Hara's ugliness. He was in his middle thirties and had already grown heavy; his head rose out of an exceptionally thick neck and his ears stuck out bizarrely from fleshy cheeks. To make matters worse, he had a bad complexion and a mouthful of decaying teeth, which he was all too slowly having replaced.

BRENDAN GILL ON JOHN O'HARA,
Here at the New Yorker

In appearance she is small and provocative, rather like a lovely naughty child, with her flashing gipsy eyes and shining black hair. There is always a sort of mockery in her eyes and about her mouth…she is not easy to know, and she appears to dislike more people than she likes.

ETHEL MANNIN ON REBECCA WEST,
Confessions and Impressions

We spent the evening in Katherine-Anne's rather barren bedroom drinking bourbon. Everyone at Yaddo has been jumping on the poor woman and she's had a nervous breakdown since I saw her in June. She seemed thoroughly chastened, quite haggard, a much more genuine and attractive person. She sat on the edge of her bed at two in the morning, her make-up worn off, her face lined and weathered, talking about lonelyness and for a moment or two I thought I saw a person through the artificiality and conceit.

JOHN CHEEVER ON KATHERINE ANNE PORTER,
The Letters of John Cheever

He was a courteous fidgety man with a rapid laugh that ended in a blend of hum, snort, and sigh, as jazz singers used to end a chorus with "Oh, yeass". He was wonderfully quick – quick in apprehension, quick to find the words he wanted, quick to move on. The prose reflected the man, except that what in the man sometimes seemed impatience was in the prose all golden speed and directness.

JOHN UPDIKE ON JOHN CHEEVER,
Odd Jobs

I do not remember having a single interesting conversation with Philip Larkin, though I spent hours and hours in his company. His first comment to my wife when he met her, having sat silently for about five minutes and surveyed our room, was: "Where do you put out your rubbish?"

A.N.WILSON ON PHILIP LARKIN,
London Evening Standard, 11 March 1993

Poets Cornered

A hyena that wrote poetry in tombs.

FRIEDRICH NIETZSCHE ON DANTE ALIGHIERI

The whole of Milton's poem [*Paradise Lost*] is such barbarous trash, so outrageously offensive to reason and to common sense that one is naturally led to wonder how it can have been tolerated by a people, amongst whom astronomy, navigation, and chemistry are understood.

WILLIAM COBBETT

His imagination resembled the wings of an ostrich. It enabled him to run, though not to soar.

THOMAS BABINGTON MACAULAY ON JOHN DRYDEN

His more ambitious works may be defined as careless thinking carefully versified.

JAMES RUSSELL LOWELL ON ALEXANDER POPE

The verses, when they were written, resembled nothing so much as spoonfuls of boiling oil, ladled out by a fiendish monkey at an upstairs window upon such of the passers-by whom the wretch had a grudge against.

LYTTON STRACHEY ON ALEXANDER POPE

An addiction to poetry is very generally the result of "an uneasy mind in an uneasy body" – Chatterton, *I* think, is mad.

LORD BYRON ON THOMAS CHATTERTON,
letter to Leigh Hunt, November 1815

No man ever walked down to posterity with so small a book under his arm.

CHARLES DICKENS ON THOMAS GRAY

Here is Johnny Keats' piss-a-bed poetry. No more Keats, I entreat; flay him alive; if some of you don't I must skin him myself; there is no bearing the drivelling idiotism of the Mankin.

LORD BYRON,
letter to John Murray, 12 October 1821

Shelley I saw once. His voice was the most obnoxious squeak I ever was tormented with, ten thousand times worse than the Laureat's [Robert Southey], whose voice is the worst part about him, except his Laureatcy.

CHARLES LAMB,

letter, 9 October 1822

What a beastly and pitiful wretch that Wordsworth... I can compare him with no one but Simonides, that flatterer of the Sycilian tyrants.

PERCY BYSSHE SHELLEY

Mrs Browning's death is rather a relief to me, I must say: no more Aurora Leighs, thank God! A woman of real Genius, I know; but what is the upshot of it all? She and her Sex had better mind the Kitchen and the Children; and perhaps the Poor; except in such things as little Novels, they only devote themselves to what Men do much better, leaving that which Men do worse or not at all.

EDWARD FITZGERALD ON
ELIZABETH BARRETT BROWNING,

letter, 15 July 1861

Can't understand Rimbaud at all.

JOSEPH CONRAD

Tennyson is a beautiful half of a poet.

RALPH WALDO EMERSON

Rilke was the greatest Lesbian poet since Sappho.

W.H.AUDEN

Thomas was an outstandingly unpleasant man, one who cheated and stole from his friends and peed on their carpets.

KINGSLEY AMIS ON DYLAN THOMAS

No one...will ever again believe in the Frost Story, the Frost myth, which includes the premises that Frost the man was kindly, forbearing, energetic, hard-working, goodneighborly, or anything but the small-minded, vindictive, ill-tempered, egotistic, cruel, and unforgiving man he was.

JAMES DICKEY ON ROBERT FROST

Oh, good. Now we can all move up one.

BRIAN PATTEN,
on hearing that W.H.Auden had died

A great second-rate poet.

MALCOLM BRADBURY ON JOHN BETJEMAN

He is a ham actor, not a poet.

ALLEN TATE ON YEVGENY YEVTUSHENKO

Praise Be!

Many of the greatest men that ever lived have written biography. Boswell was one of the smallest men that ever lived, and he has beaten them all.

THOMAS BABINGTON MACAULAY

Poe is the only impeccable writer. He was never mistaken.

PAUL VALÉRY

He is one of the new and far better generation of your writers. The smell of your beeches and hemlocks is upon him; your own broad prairies are in his soul; and if you travel away inland into his deep and noble nature, you will hear the far roar of his Niagara.

HERMAN MELVILLE ON NATHANIEL HAWTHORNE

The death of Mme Sand has also distressed me greatly, very greatly... She loved us both – you especially – that was only natural. What a heart of gold she had! Such an absence of all low, petty or false sentiments — what a good fellow she was and what a fine woman! And now all of that is there, in the horrible relentless hole in the ground, silent, stupid — and it doesn't even know what it is it's devouring!

IVAN TURGENEV ON GEORGE SAND,

letter to Gustave Flaubert, 18 June 1876

Emerson is more than a brilliant fellow. Be his stuff begged, borrowed, or stolen, or of his own domestic manufacture, he is an uncommon man. Swear he is a humbug — then is he no common humbug.

HERMAN MELVILLE ON RALPH WALDO EMERSON

That Walt Whitman, of whom I wrote to you, is the most interesting fact to me at present. I have just read his second edition (which he gave me), and it has done me more good than any reading for a long time... There are two or three pieces in the book which are disagreeable, to say the least; simply sensual. He does not celebrate love at all. It is as if the beasts spoke. I think that men have not been ashamed of themselves without reason. No doubt there have always been dens where such deeds were unblushingly recited, and it is no merit to compete with their inhabitants. But even on this side he has spoken more truth than any American or modern that I know.

HENRY DAVID THOREAU,

letter, 7 December 1856

Ah, what a beautiful, magnificent man: modest and quiet like a girl. He even walks like a girl. He's simply wonderful.

LEO TOLSTOY ON ANTON CHEKHOV

There is no end of Kipling in my work. I have even quoted him. I would never possibly have written anywhere near the way I did had Kipling never been.

JACK LONDON

I don't suppose any writer was ever more completely the professional. He has an accurate and fearless appraisal of his own gifts, the greatest of which is not literary at all, but is rather that neat and inexorable perception of character and motive which belongs to the great judge or the great diplomat... He never makes you catch your breath or lose your head, because he never loses his. I doubt that he ever wrote a line which seemed fresh from creation, and many lesser writers have. But he will outlast them all with ease, because he is without folly or silliness. He would have made a great Roman.

RAYMOND CHANDLER ON SOMERSET MAUGHAM,
letter to Hamish Hamilton, 5 January 1950

But as for living novelists, I suppose E.M.Forster is the best, not knowing what that is, but at least he's a semi-finalist, wouldn't you think? Somerset Maugham once said to me: "We have a novelist over here, E.M.Forster, though I don't suppose he's familiar to you." Well, I could have kicked him. Did he think I carried a papoose on my back? Why, I'd go on my hands and knees to get to Forster.

DOROTHY PARKER,

Paris Review interview

Better than anyone else, he told the truth about his time, the first half of the twentieth century. He was a professional. He wrote honestly and well.

JOHN O'HARA ON HIMSELF

(the self-written epitaph on his gravestone at Princeton)

Easily the most interesting English writer of the last half century.

GORE VIDAL ON ANTHONY BURGESS

I deeply admire Bellow. He is Jewish-American and I'm not, his vision is shaped by intellectual funds and cultural conflict that are not mine. But I have a strong sense of oblique intimacy with him. I've always felt a terrific radiation from his books.

MALCOLM BRADBURY

Up Staged

Shakespeare's name, you may depend on it, stands absurdly too high and will go down. He had no invention as to stories, none whatever. He took all his plots from old novels, and threw their stories into a dramatic shape, at as little expense of thought as you or I could turn his plays back again into prose tales. That he threw over whatever he did write some flashes of genius, nobody can deny: but this was all.

LORD BYRON,

letter to James Hogg, March 1814

Shakespeare never had six lines without a fault.

SAMUEL JOHNSON

The undisputed fame enjoyed by Shakespeare as a writer is like every other lie, a great evil.

LEO TOLSTOY

With the single exception of Homer, there is no eminent writer, not even Sir Walter Scott, whom I can despise so entirely as I despise Shakespeare when I measure my mind against his.

GEORGE BERNARD SHAW

I don't know if Bacon wrote the works of Shakespeare, but if he did not, he missed the opportunity of his life.

JAMES BARRIE

In truth, Wycherley's indecency is protected against the critics as a skunk is protected against the hunters. It is safe because it is too filthy to handle, and too noisome even to approach.

THOMAS BABINGTON MACAULAY ON WILLIAM WYCHERLEY

Cibber! write all thy Verses upon Glasses,
The only way to save 'em from our Arses.

ALEXANDER POPE ON COLLEY CIBBER

Mr Coward is credited with the capacity to turn out these very highly polished pieces of writing in an incredibly short time. And if rumour and the illustrated weeklies are to be believed, he writes his plays in a flowered dressing-gown and before breakfast. But what I want to know is what kind of work he intends to do after breakfast, when he is clothed and in his right mind.

JAMES AGATE ON NOËL COWARD

Mr Kaufman spent a good deal of his time, particularly in the late afternoons, stretched out full length on the floor, and it was usually at one of these unwary moments when he was at his lowest ebb and stretched helplessly below me, that I would stand over him and deliver my captivating compendium of the day's work. Something like a small moan, which I misinterpreted as agreement, would escape from his lips and he would turn his head away from the sight of my face, much the way a man whose arm is about to be jabbed with a needle averts his gaze to spare himself the extra pain of seeing the needle descend.

MOSS HART ON GEORGE S. KAUFMAN,

Act One

Brecht was an admirable man, in the sense that one surely must admire someone who lived in a Communist country but took out Austrian citizenship, kept his money in a Swiss bank, and hedged his bets when he was dying by sending for the priest, just in case.

W.H.AUDEN

Having recently seen *St Joan* in London and *Caesar and Cleopatra* in Sydney, it is clearer to me than ever that Shaw is the most fraudulent, inept writer of Victorian melodramas ever to gull a timid critic or fool a dull public. He writes like a Pakistani who had learned English when he was twelve years old in order to become a chartered accountant.

JOHN OSBORNE,

letter to the Guardian, 1977

I remember coming across him at the Grand Canyon and finding him peevish and refusing to admire it or even look at it properly. He was jealous of it.

J.B.PRIESTLEY ON GEORGE BERNARD SHAW,
Thoughts in the Wilderness

Drunkenness with him was more a state of mind than a physical condition. He had to be drunk in order to carry with an air of insouciance the load of phoneyness he had piled on his own back.

MALCOLM MUGGERIDGE ON BRENDAN BEHAN,
Observer, 25 July 1970

I fear that Mr John Osborne is not so talented as he has been made out to be... I cannot believe that this writer, the first of the "angry young men", was ever really angry at all. Dissatisfied, perhaps, and certainly envious and, to a degree, talented, but no more than that. No leader of thought or ideas, a conceited, calculating young man blowing a little trumpet.

NOËL COWARD,
Diary, 5 May 1959

Word Bites

A crawling and disgusting parasite, a base scoundrel, and pander to unnatural passions.

WILLIAM COBBETT ON VIRGIL

Our language sank under him.

JOSEPH ADDISON ON JOHN MILTON

Rousseau, Sir, is a very bad man. I would sooner sign a sentence for his transportation, than that of any felon who has gone from the Old Bailey these many years. Yes, I should like to have him work in the plantations.

SAMUEL JOHNSON

Goethe is the greatest genius who has lived for a century, and the greatest ass who has lived for three.

THOMAS CARLYLE

He can comprehend but one idea at a time, and that is always an extreme one; because he will neither listen to, nor tolerate any thing that can disturb or moderate the petulance of his self-opinion.

WILLIAM HAZLITT ON ROBERT SOUTHEY

He not only overflowed with learning, but stood in the slop.

SYDNEY SMITH ON THOMAS BABINGTON MACAULAY

[Edward] Bulwer-Lytton I detest. He is the very pimple of the age's humbug.

NATHANIEL HAWTHORNE

She is above all and more than anything else, of a cow-like stupidity.

CHARLES BAUDELAIRE ON GEORGE SAND

Carlyle is the same old sausage, fizzing and spluttering in his own grease.

HENRY JAMES

It was very good of God to let Carlyle and Mrs Carlyle marry one another and so make only two people miserable instead of four.

SAMUEL BUTLER

I could readily see in Emerson a gaping flaw. It was the insinuation that had he lived in those days when the world was made, he might have offered some valuable suggestions.

HERMAN MELVILLE

A gap-toothed and hoary-headed ape, carried at first into notice on the shoulder of Carlyle...who now in his dotage spits and chatters from a dirtier perch of his own finding and fouling.

ALGERNON CHARLES SWINBURNE
ON RALPH WALDO EMERSON

A perfect leper and a mere sodomite.

RALPH WALDO EMERSON
ON ALGERNON CHARLES SWINBURNE

This individual of doubtful sex, with a ham actor's language, and tall stories.

EDMOND GONCOURT ON OSCAR WILDE

[His] method of literary piracy was on the lines of the robber Cacus, who dragged stolen cows backwards by the tails into his cavern so that their hooveprints might not lead to the detection of the robbery.

GEORGE MOORE ON OSCAR WILDE

A grocer temporarily installed in the place of an artist. His novels are unbearable to a sensitive spirit.

OSCAR WILDE ON GEORGE MOORE

James is developing, but he will never arrive at passion, I fear.

OSCAR WILDE ON HENRY JAMES

He is neither first rate, nor second rate, nor tenth rate. He is just his horrible unique self.

GEORGE BERNARD SHAW ON FRANK HARRIS

Chesterton is like a vile scum on a pond... I believe he creates a milieu in which art is impossible.

EZRA POUND

If it must be Thomas, let it be Mann, and if it must be Wolfe let it be Nero, but never let it be Thomas Wolfe.

PETER DE VRIES

Just a New Jersey Nero who mistook his pinafore for a toga.

EDNA FERBER ON ALEXANDER WOOLLCOTT

English literature's performing flea.

SEAN O'CASEY ON P.G. WODEHOUSE

He would not blow his nose without moralising on the state of the handkerchief industry.

CYRIL CONNOLLY ON GEORGE ORWELL

I don't like a man that takes the short way home.

WILLIAM FAULKNER,
on hearing that Ernest Hemingway had shot himself, 1961

She looked like Lady Chatterley above the waist, and the gamekeeper below.

CYRIL CONNOLLY ON VITA SACKVILLE-WEST

The stupid person's idea of the clever person.

ELIZABETH BOWEN ON ALDOUS HUXLEY

That old lady is a crashing bore.

DOROTHY PARKER ON SOMERSET MAUGHAM

Every word she writes is a lie, including "and" and "the".

MARY McCARTHY ON LILLIAN HELLMAN

He'd be all right if he took his finger out of his mouth.

HAROLD ROBBINS ON TRUMAN CAPOTE

I had always found Graves's character to be exactly divided, half and half, between schoolboy and schoolmaster – to me, not a very attractive combination.

OSBERT SITWELL ON ROBERT GRAVES

When *The Naked and the Dead* appeared, I thought someone the size of Dickens was among us; I had not allowed for the fact that Mailer was an American.

KINGSLEY AMIS

Salinger is everyone's favourite. I seem to be alone in finding him no more than the greatest mind ever to stay in prep school.

NORMAN MAILER

Bellow is a Ukrainian-Canadian, I believe. It is painful to watch him trying to pick his way between the unidiomatic on the one hand and the affected on the other.

KINGSLEY AMIS

Mr Raphael has many opinions about books that he has not actually read. You'll see him at his glittering best in *The Times*, in his obituary of Gore Vidal (date to come).

GORE VIDAL ON FREDERIC RAPHAEL

ACKNOWLEDGEMENTS

Permission from authors and publishers to quote from the following works is gratefully acknowledged: *Pages from the Goncourt Journal* (edited & translated by Robert Baldick), Oxford University Press 1962; Bertrand Russell *Autobiography 1914-44*, copyright © Bertrand Russell Peace Foundation Ltd; *Exile's Return* by Malcolm Cowley, copyright © 1934, 1935, 1941, 1951 Malcolm Cowley, Viking Penguin, a division of Penguin Books USA Inc; *Kiss Hollywood Goodbye* by Anita Loos, The Anita Loos Trusts; *Margin Released* by J B Priestley, Wm Heinemann 1962; Profile of Malcolm Lowry by Martin Amis (*The Independent* 12.12.93), courtesy the Peters Fraser & Dunlop Group Ltd; *Selected Letters of Dylan Thomas* (J M Dent 1985), courtesy David Higham Associates; Humphrey Carpenter; *Will This Do?* by Auberon Waugh (Century 1991), courtesy the Peters Fraser & Dunlop Group Ltd; *Homage to Daniel Shays* by Gore Vidal, Random House Inc 1972; *Novelists in Interview* (Methuen) copyright © John Haffenden 1985, courtesy Curtis Brown, London Ltd on behalf of the author; *Flaubert and Turgenev: A Friendship in Letters* (ed Barbara Beaumont), Athlone Press Ltd; interviews with James Thurber, Vladimir Nabokov, Dorothy Parker, *The Paris Review*, 1957; *Enemies of Promise* by Cyril Connolly, copyright © 1938, 1948 Cyril Connolly, courtesy Rogers, Coleridge & White Ltd; *Essays, Speeches & Public Letters of William Faulkner* (ed James B Meriwether), Random House Inc; Norman Mailer's introduction to *Genius and Lust: the major writings of Henry Miller*, Grove/Atlantic Inc, 1976; Irwin Shaw review, copyright © 1946 by The New York Times Company, reprinted by permission; Leslie Fiedler's article "Irwin Shaw: Adultery, the Last Politics" reprinted from *Commentary*, July 1956; *Capote: A Biography* by Gerald Clarke, copyright © Gerald Clarke 1988, reproduced by permission of Hamish Hamilton Ltd; Julie Burchill review, courtesy *The Spectator*, London; *Journals of Arnold Bennett* by permission of A P Watt Ltd on behalf of Mme V M Eldin; *Diaries of Virginia Woolf* (Volume V), Chatto & Windus/Hogarth Press; *Diaries of Evelyn Waugh* (ed Michael Davie), Weidenfeld & Nicolson 1976, courtesy the Peters Fraser & Dunlop Group Ltd; *Noël Coward Diaries* (ed Graham Payn & Sheridan Morley), Weidenfeld & Nicolson 1982; *The Journals* of John Cheever (Jonathan Cape 1991), courtesy Aitken, Stone & Wylie Ltd; *Conversations with Capote* by Lawrence Grobel (New American Library), copyright © Lawrence Grobel, courtesy Sterling Lord Literistic Inc; *The Fourteenth Chronicle: Letters & Diaries of John Dos Passos*, Harvard Common Press 1973; *While Rome Burns* by Alexander Woollcott, copyright © 1943 Alexander Woollcott, renewed © 1962 Joseph P Hennessey, by permission Viking Penguin, a division of Penguin Books USA Inc; Auberon Waugh on P G Wodehouse, courtesy *New Statesman & Society*; *Advertisements for Myself* by Norman Mailer, courtesy Aitken, Stone & Wylie Ltd; *Taken Care Of* by Edith Sitwell (Hutchinson 1965), courtesy David Higham Ltd; *Midnight Oil* by V S Pritchett (Chatto & Windus 1971), courtesy the Peters Fraser & Dunlop Group Ltd; *Six Men* by Alistair Cooke, Random House Inc; *World Within World* by Stephen Spender (Hamish Hamilton 1951), courtesy the Peters Fraser & Dunlop Group Ltd; *Here at the New Yorker* by Brendan Gill, Random House Inc; *The Letters Of John Cheever* – ed Benjamin Cheever (Jonathan Cape 1989), courtesy Aitken, Stone & Wylie; *Odd Jobs* by John Updike, copyright © John Updike 1991, Random House Inc/Penguin Books Ltd; A N Wilson on Philip Larkin, copyright © *London Evening Standard*/Solo; *Chekhov* by Henri Troyat (trans Michael Henry Heim, copyright © 1986 E P Dutton), courtesy Dutton Signet, a division of Penguin Books USA Inc; *Raymond Chandler Speaking* (ed Dorothy Gardiner & Katherine Sorley Walker), Hamish Hamilton 1962, copyright © Helga Green Literary Agency 1962; *Act One* by Moss Hart, Random House Inc; *The Life of a Poet* by Charles Osborne (Rainbird 1979), copyright © Charles Osborne 1979, courtesy Penguin Books Ltd; John Osborne for permission to quote from his letter to the *Guardian*; *Thoughts in the Wilderness* by J B Priestley, Wm Heinemann 1962; Malcolm Muggeridge on Brendan Behan, courtesy David Higham Associates; *Laughter in the Next Room* by Osbert Sitwell, copyright © Frank Magro Esq, courtesy David Higham Associates; *A View from the Diners Club* by Gore Vidal, Random House Inc.